THE
Archive Photographs
SERIES

ST AUSTELL

Members of the St Austell Old Cornwall Society. The secretary Arthur Rowett on the left, with the president on the right, are inspecting the remains of an old well which was revealed after clearing debris from the Fore Street fire in 1940. The St Austell Old Cornwall Society was founded in 1925. The first few meetings were held in the Liberal Club, Town Hall and Miss Hawley's school room at Moorland House in Fore Street, with Dr H.N. Wright of Cuddra as president. The 'Old Cornwall Society' is still flourishing to this day.

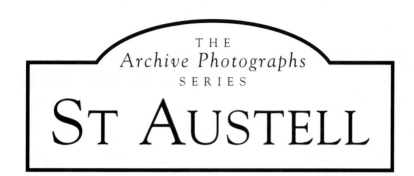

THE
Archive Photographs
SERIES

ST AUSTELL

Compiled by
Valerie Brokenshire

For Norman
Happy Memories of your
Visit to Trenanen.
June 1997.
            Valerie

CHALFORD

First published 1997
Copyright © Valerie Brokenshire, 1997

The Chalford Publishing Company
St Mary's Mill, Chalford,
Stroud, Gloucestershire, GL6 8NX

ISBN 0 7524 0787 2

Typesetting and origination by
The Chalford Publishing Company
Printed in Great Britain by
Redwood Books, Trowbridge

Dedicated to Dr A.L. Rowse C.H.
who has always loved his home town
and his native Cornwall.

Contents

Acknowledgements   6

Introduction   7

1.   Street Scenes   9

2.   Businesses and Shops   23

3.   Buildings   35

4.   The Parish Church and Chapels   47

5.   Processions and Occasions   59

6.   General Views and Approaches   67

7.   Roads, Transport and China Clay   75

8.   Organisations and Clubs   89

9.   The District   101

10. The Coast   111

Acknowledgements

In compiling this book my main debt of gratitude is to my good friend, Brian Jacob who encouraged me to begin by offering assistance with the captions and the research. Brian also introduced me to Fred Elton who provided many of the included illustrations. In addition, the cover photograph is also from the Fred Elton collection.

I am most grateful to my 'Old Cornwall Society' friends Robert Evans and Sam Edyvean whose initial interest and support introduced me to the idea.

To all the other St Austell people who have loaned photographs, bill headings and other records, I express my sincere thanks:
H.R.A. (Dolphy) Vivian; Mr and Mrs C. Petherick; Joyce and Melville Robins; Bill Champion, Ray Clemo; W.H. Trevains; H. Mills; Bill Jago; Michael Treleaven; St Austell Fire Brigade; Archie Smith; B. Bray; Roy Dutch; D. Tregilgas; Mr and Mrs J. Luke; Cornwall Record Office: Copyright reserved for printed billheads: CN 3441/4/24 CN 3441/4/8 CN 33441/4/6 CN 3441/4/1.

Special thanks to my friend Carol Folley for the unenviable task of putting the finished draft onto computer, with such expertise.

Lastly, but certainly not least, my special regard for Dr A.L. Rowse C.H. who, despite his failing health, has provided numerous facts with instant recall. His encouragement has always been constant.

St Austell's Coat of Arms.

Introduction

St Austell, situated about two miles from the south coast has developed from 'a poore village with nothing notable but the Paroch Chirch' according to John Leland, an early traveller in Cornwall between the years 1534 to 1543.

St Austell, Austol or Austle, a Celtic missionary saint was a younger companion to St Mewan. They settled within a mile of each other, St Mewan still the neighbouring parish. Carew in 1602 describes Trenans Austel, indicating that the stream flowing through the valley in Trenance was the first place St Austell chose to settle.

At Menacuddle, a little higher up the valley from Trenance, a hollow in the perpendicular rock became known as St Austell Well and the ancient baptistry which still stands there has a permanent spring and stream of water flowing out of the rock face. It is likely that somewhere in this area a small cell within an enclosure was built possibly on the southern slopes, the site of the future town, and later a baptistry or small chantry chapel building which was replaced by a parish church. In 1294, a record from the Tywardreath priory notes 'Ecclesia de Sancto Austolo'.

The development of trade and business around the church is the history of many Cornish towns. Celia Fiennes in 1695 called St Austell 'a little market town' and about a hundred years later, Richard Pococke named it a 'little tinning town'. By the 1800s, W.G. Maton records that the place only has the church to recommend it, but that 'there are large blowing houses at the western extremity', indicating the growth and prosperity introduced since the discovery of tin and copper deposits.

By 1833, St Austell was defined as a Coinage Town, indicating its importance within the tin area and from the time of Oliver Cromwell a market charter had been granted as a reward to one of his followers called May, who had a seat near the town. The granting of the market charter was soon followed by that of two annual fairs, for the sale of livestock, coarse woollens and other manufactured goods. Stockdale in 1824, records that the people there were 'industrious and thriving'.

The next development included the transition to the china clay trade, with the area around the town producing some of the finest clay deposits in the world. The town developed and grew in all directions during this and fine houses, avenues and buildings were added to the main streets, a symbol of advancing prosperity. Trade in the town developed apace and the transportation of the china clay by horse-drawn wagons through the streets engendered an aura of thriving trade and industry throughout the nineteenth and early twentieth century.

From St Austell itself, the radius of its prosperity extended to Pentewan, by the railway from the West Bridge area to the docks, and to Charlestown, through the export of china clay on coasting vessels to other parts of Britain from the enclosed dock or inner harbour.

The villages around St Austell were thriving communities too, and the importance of the town was obvious on market days, Saturdays and feast days when the population from these areas congregated in the streets and the shops thrived with trade. Canon Hammond in 1897 called it 'the most flourishing town in the county'.

There have been many changes in the town during the last four decades, with the emphasis on large out-of-town stores cornering the shopping trade. The town is no longer the hub of commerce it once was, but the observant visitor, who looks above the plate glass shop fronts, can still trace many architectural features illustrated in this book.

We now have pedestrianisation in Fore Street, Aylmer Square and Vicarage Place with the traffic confined to the periphery of the town.

Valerie Brokenshire
St Austell
March 1997

W. ORCHARD
PHOTOGRAPHER
8, High Cross Street
ST AUSTELL

ALL NEGATIVES CAREFULLY KEPT N°.............
ENLARGEMENTS MADE FROM ANY
PHOTOGRAPHS TO ANY SIZE AND PAINTED
IN OIL, WATER COLOUR OR CRAYON.

One

Street Scenes

The street plan of St Austell has not changed much in the last hundred years. Originally, the turnpike road from Truro to London entered St Austell over the old bridge at the bottom of West Hill, through Fore Street, Church Street and up East Hill as it left the town. Truro Road and Bodmin Road were not added until the middle of the nineteenth century.

The main new street, Trinity Street, was built during the 1960s to relieve traffic problems connected with the growth of the tourist industry. The church is the focal centre of the town and dominates the area and many of the streets lead in this direction.

A bill heading of E. Kellaway & Son, Saddlers and Harness manufacturers.

Left: Church Street in the 1890s. At the head of this street was the White Lion, a beer and eating house, the sign well displayed over the door. In 1873, under the churchyard wall, there were three small shop premises in the area known as the Bull Ring. These were Wm H. Hammer the photographer, Sam Truscott the saddler and Walter Wherry the beer retailer. The Georgian two-storeyed house on the extreme right was owned by Charles Rashleigh, who built the harbour at Charlestown and developed the shipping trade there.

Below: The old Bull Ring area of the town showing the Coode's Bank, built in 1898 and designed by Silvanus Trevail, in the area where the White Lion had stood. The curved building opposite was the Corn Exchange, built in 1859 at the head of Hotel Road. It became the district Food Office during the Second World War. The ancient White Hart coaching inn had moved from Fore Street and with another added storey occupied the Charles Rashleigh town house.

The end of Fore Street looking towards the West End of the town, shows where the Bodmin Road met the turnpike from Truro. Tidy's corner shop was a wholesale and retail cigar and tobacco merchant as well as catering for some sporting equipment. Note the sign outside for cricket stumps and bat. This area was known as Tidy's Corner. The building at the top of Truro Road was the Globe Hotel, with Warne's, the printer's occupying the ground floor. The butcher, F.W. May had a thriving business in the town alongside the Liberal Club and delivered throughout the surrounding area as well.

Fore Street from the junction of Bodmin Road. The lower left hand shop was the first W.H. Smith & Son in the town, before moving to the premises where the Kitchen Corner is now, at the junction of Fore Street and Church Street. The glass and china shop of Harvey Bros is opposite.

Looking down Truro Road from Tidy's Corner, the shop front of May the butcher is on the left. The Globe Hotel, at the head of Truro Road was next to the Assembly Rooms which was built in 1846 and designed by Silvanus Trevail. Notice the large bay window jutting out well onto the pavement with the Cadbury's advertisement in the end window.

Still towards the western end of the town, this view of Fore Street shows a very narrow part. The delivery trap is waiting outside George Hawkes, the ironmonger, at No. 27. Galvanised baths and various pieces of ironmongery are hanging in the doorway. The local newspapers advertised on the end wall are the *Daily Mercury*, *Evening Herald* and *The Guardian*.

Fore Street, St. Austell.

At the early part of this century, Fore Street would have looked like this. This view, which is free of traffic and people, shows the town house of the Flamank family, one of the last private residences on the street level. Architectural details are clear on the first storey over the shops and span over different eras, ending in the view of the tiered Tudor-style building with its porch extending over the pavement.

St. Austell, Fore Street.

Fore Street in another early 1900s view, with the Caroline porch of the town house belonging to the Tremayne family. This later became Miners the pork butcher's shop and is now Warrens the bakery. On the left hand side, Hodge the seedsman was listed in 1910 as proprietor of the Sun Inn at No. 13 Market Street, and a nursery seedsman.

Fore Street, *c.* 1911. A view from the same angle as the previous photograph but at a later date.

As the century progressed so did the prosperity of the china clay trade. The clay wagons, with high-mounded loads, trundled through the main thoroughfare of the town on their way from the clay area around St Stephen-in-Brannel to the port of Charlestown. Traffic was two-way and in the narrow streets the high sided wagons must have caused many problems. Often there was a line of wagons waiting at the bottom of East Hill for an extra horse to make the ascent.

14

Fore Street in an 1890s photograph showing the Temperance Hotel facing Market Square in the centre background. The top-hatted gentleman, with pin stripe trousers, striding impatiently through the street, seems bent on important business. Note the shiny canvas or rolls of linoleum arranged attractively to catch the passing trade, in the lower right hand shop doorway.

FORE STREET, S.^T AUSTELL, Christmas 189 2

J. Carlyon Esqre

To Thomas Mann,

General & Furnishing Ironmonger,

PLUMBER, GAS FITTER, TIN, IRON & ZINC WORKER.

SHEFFIELD CUTLERY & ELECTRO PLATE, REGISTER & RUMFORD GRATES.
PUMPS. WATER CLOSETS, GAS CHANDELIERS, IRON AND BRASS BEDSTEADS, &c.
A LARGE ASSORTMENT OF CARPENTERS' TOOLS. MARDONS' BRISTOL.

Market Street in an early view this century, which shows the building known today as the Old Manor House, with the first St Austell Co-operative Society on the ground floor. On the corner of Menacuddle Street was Rosevear's the outfitters, costumier and milliner, and next to it the Queen's Head which together with the White Hart, were the two most important hotels in the town. The crowd, mostly young boys and men are assembled at what was commonly known as 'Fool's Corner'.

Church Street, c. 1905. Three very old shop frontages of Juleff, Reed and the Golden Lion pub can be seen. Reed, the jeweller, was also a goldsmith and optician. There is a giant pair of spectacles angled out over his shop window. Pascoe and Piper, a gentlemen's outfitter and tailor in Victoria Place was next to Stockers, the prosperous ironmongers and plumbers.

A view down Market Square with Walter Hicks' public house next to the Sun Inn, now O'Callaghan's, and the sign of the Queen's Head jutting out in the line further down past the market house. The granite war memorial erected after the First World War is a fine example of a Cornish Celtic cross.

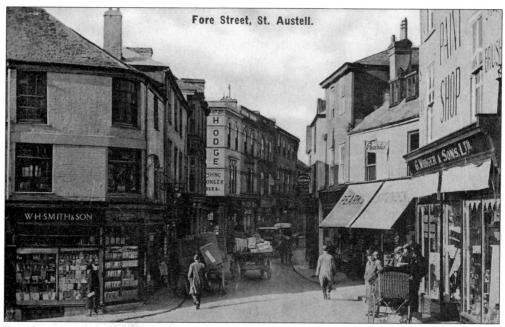

Fore Street in the 1940s. The photographer must have stood in the roadway outside the parish church to take this photograph. W.H. Smith occupied the corner site on the junction with Church Street and traded there for over forty years. The shop, formerly Rosevear's, now houses Widger & Son. Several well-loaded delivery wagons wait in Fore Street. The post office wicker hand cart delivering town mail is on the extreme right hand side.

Fore Street, outside Woolworths looking towards the West End in the 1950s. The café and restaurant of Richards and Dyer, Sydney Grose, Eustace, Eastman and Hepworth were all names in the town which survived for many years.

The same view about forty years earlier, with Reuben Nicholas Rogers at No. 28 Fore Street as the owner of the grocery store. This curve of the main street of St Austell looks very similar today and strangely enough is still traffic free as shown in these two photographs, because Fore Street is now pedestrianised.

Looking westward from the middle of Fore Street, *c.* 1935. This photograph shows the façade of Thomas Grose's old shop, linen and woollen draper, which was later re-built as the Co-operative Society. The building was totally destroyed by a fire in 1940. The early Woolworths is on the left hand side of the street. Boots with its circulating library, and Timothy White opposite, flanked the street alongside Hodge's the ironmonger, famous for its copper kettle hanging outside which dated 1830.

Grant's Walk, a small walkway leading off the Bodmin Road and along the back of Fore Street, contained some fine residential houses. On the left are the premises of W. & T. Sanders, printers and the publishers of the *St Austell Star* newspaper. The boy with the wooden wheelbarrow with the iron wheels dates the photograph. He was possibly collecting the horse manure for the garden.

Fore Street in the 1950s. This more modern view of Fore Street shows Timothy Whites the chemist, opposite Boots in the era before they amalgamated. The Clifden Grill was on the first floor but it moved in the 1960s to Aylmer Square in the new town centre, again occupying a floor over shop premises. The Millard family business closed in 1995.

Fore Street viewed from the church area in the 1950s. Peark's on the corner was only one of a number of flourishing grocery businesses at this time. Sited outside the shop and set in the pavement was the Mengu stone. This ancient boundary marker of the three manors Trenance, Treverbyn and Tewington, was also used as a proclamation stone. It was moved to the foot of the church tower and set in the ground for safe keeping when the Alliance and Leicester Building Society modernised the premises. Traffic in Fore Street at this time was still two-way. The car with the number NCV 731 was a Humber Pullman, one of a fleet of taxis which belonged to Percy Cocks.

Trinity Street. During the early 1960s when the road widening scheme and formation of Trinity Street was planned, this old established business of J. & A. Phillips, with its prime site at the end of Fore Street was demolished. The higher shop had a tiled floor arcade with plate glass display windows.

Road widening in progress in the Trinity Street and the West Hill area. Burton Place was demolished but left its name to Burton House. The backs of the shops along Fore Street to Hawke's are visible.

At the lower end of East Hill and on the corner of Hotel Road and Church Street was the Corn Exchange building. The lower storey shown here housed the second Cornwall County Library from 1945 to 1960. The first one was situated in the YMCA building in Victoria Square where Arthur Rowett was the librarian.

A similar view of the lower end of East Hill showing the Corn Exchange with its date stone of 1859 on the front. This handsome granite building was used by the Ministry of Supply during the Second World War as a food office and the store managed by 'Chirpy' Richards. It was demolished by Western Excavating on 19 December 1960 as part of a road widening scheme for modern traffic.

Two

Businesses and Shops

There were many family businesses in St Austell following through three or four generations, with the same name above the shop door. Grose, Warne and Vivian were family names in this category.

From a small market town, St Austell developed with the prosperity of the tin mines and subsequently the china clay productions, so that by 1870 the main streets were well endowed with the principal shops befitting a busy and thriving community. The Post Office Directory of 1873 suggests there were nine linen and woollen drapers in Fore Street alone.

There were also hat manufacturers, cabinet makers, saddlers, milliners and tailors to supply the needs of the surrounding populace. On Fridays the town would be busy all day long as this was market day while on Saturday the shops stayed open until 10 pm plying their trade.

A bill heading from Henry Hodge, a seedsman and nurseryman, 1893. The bill included 14oz of carrot seed, 62lb of peas, as well as 50 Scotch firs and 15 standard apple trees for the gardens and grounds at Tregrehan House.

J.F. Frost's music shop on the corner of Fore Street and Bodmin Road was a combination of music and furnishings as advertised. Notice the horned gramophones in the window display a feature of the times. The business later moved to East Hill when the Vivian brothers moved to this shop.

The two Vivian brothers standing outside the newly appointed shops. There is a wonderful display of pocket and fob watches with mantel clocks arranged on shelves. The four men managed both shop premises which were crammed full of goods. Outside the shop are Jack Vivian, Ted Blake, Harry Vivian and William Vivian.

The same shop as shown in the previous photograph with the two premises combined as one gentleman's outfitters, shown here in the 1940s. Harry Vivian ran the shop with the assistance of his son H.R.A. (Dolphy) Vivian. The shop finally closed in 1980 after a long span of catering for all the men's clothing needs in many a local household. There was always a chair to sit down on while waiting to be served and personal service was guaranteed with courtesy of paramount importance.

The chemist shop of William Alex Masters at No. 4 Fore Street. In 1873, it was known as the Samson Dunn chemist, Mr Masters is standing in the entrance. He was an excellent chemist and was often consulted by the public for remedies, instead of the doctor, to avoid paying the doctor's fees.

W.B. Luke of No. 12 Fore Street in 1898. This is one of the oldest existing photographs of a Fore Street shop. Notice the antiquated styles of all five windows, especially the overhanging one above the workshop entrance arch. In 1873, the premises had belonged to Andrew James booksellers, stationers and printers. William Luke continued this business and was also listed as a newsagent. He is standing in the shop entrance with his four workmen in printers' aprons alongside him.

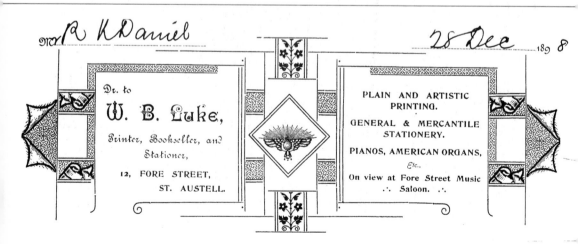

Mr Luke's bill heading which included printing 150 posters for sale of stock at Tregrehan.

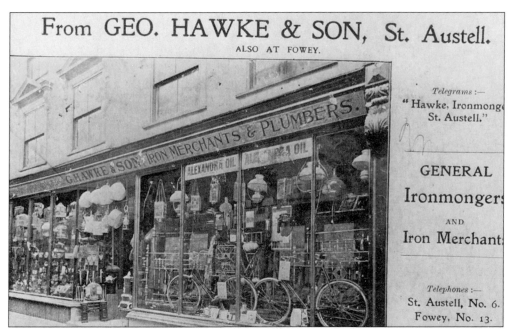

From GEO. HAWKE & SON, St. Austell.

ALSO AT FOWEY.

Telegrams :—
" Hawke, Ironmonge
St. Austell."

GENERAL

Ironmonger

AND

Iron Merchant

Telephones :—
St. Austell, No. 6.
Fowey, No. 13.

George Hawke & Son's premises at No. 37 Fore Street in 1910. In 1873, it was formerly an ironmonger's shop belonging to Bennetts & Co. It had two display windows and was like an 'Aladdin's cave' with merchandise jammed into the available space. This included gents' and ladies' bicycles, iron bedsteads and paraffin lamps. Note the early telephone number and the branch at Fowey.

J. Lanyon ran this linen and woollen draper's business in 1873. By 1910, A. J. Lanyon carried on the family's trade. This was one of the nine such premises in Fore Street and emphasised the importance of household sewing and dressmaking necessities.

This shop premises of William Box was at Nos 2 and 3 Church Street and had formerly belonged to Nettle and Box, grocer and merchant. It was a considerably high class type of grocer, dealing also in foreign wines and spirits and catering for the gentry of the area. The Carlyons of Tregrehan and the Sawles of Penrice were valued customers. The staff outside were, from left to right: Arthur Ash, William Lemin, Bill Dingle, Maud Chesterfield, Fred Pooley, Ern Rowe, Reg Michael and Frank Golley the errand boy.

2 & 3 Church Street,

St. Austell, Xmas. 1892

G R G Carlyon Esq.

BO.T OF WILLIAM BOX,

Family Grocer.

AGENT FOR W.& A.GILBEY, WINE IMPORTERS & DISTILLERS,

BASS & IND COOPE'S BOTTLED ALES & GUINNESS'S STOUT.

Interest charged on all overdue A/c.ts

NO CHRISTMAS BOXES GIVEN.

E.R. Hugo's premises in Truro Road.
Mr Hugo combined a business of selling
dairy produce, sweets and ice cream with
Lyon's cakes, Fyffe's bananas and
Cadbury's chocolate. Note the early
types of vending machines in the shop
doorway. Beech Nut chewing gum was
sold here for 1d. Mr Hugo, with his hand
on his hip, is standing in the butcher's
premises next door, with the delivery
man and his bicycle outside on the
pavement. The site is now occupied by
Clemow's hairdressing salon.

This scarcely remembered alley way in St Austell led from Fore Street, around the jeweller's at No. 29 to Aylmer Place, which later became Aylmer Square in the 1960s. The little bridge connected the jeweller's premises to the workrooms across the alley in the house opposite. The small panes of glass visible to the left of the first floor window were once part of a partition leading upstairs from the shop floor and which contained some medieval glass panels. The motorbike is an Ariel Leader of 1960s vintage.

No. 29 Fore Street, St Austell. In 1873 it was owned by T. Bray, a linen draper but was purchased by F. Whetter, jeweller and optician sometime before 1910. A wonderful array of mantel and marble case clocks adorned the upper shelves, with rings, fob watches and gold chains crammed together below.

Fred Nicholls was indentured for five years with Mr F. Whetter and learnt his trade at No. 29 Fore Street, subsequently buying the business from Mr Whetter's widow sometime during the First World War. The year is 1968, the lady standing in the doorway is Miss Nicholls, Fred's daughter, with Leonard Davey on her right and George Walker on her left, who both worked for the family in the workshops. The Nicholls' business also included the winding and maintenance of clocks in the large country houses like Penrice and Caerhayes. This would take a whole Saturday, travelling around in the area in a pony and trap. As in many instances, the family lived on the shop premises. The grating situated at pavement level was the window to the kitchen. St Austell people used to comment that when saffron was baked, the aroma wafted up into the street.

In 1893, one of the well-established and flourishing linen and woollen drapers in the town was Thomes Grose & Co. It was still there in Fore Street in 1910. In the 1930s, the premises moved further along the street and in the 1960s, Sydney Grose opened another shop in the approach to the new town centre. Note the sign on the end wall marking another of St Austell's old corners, Chandos Place, with the Bluebird Café at the lower end near to the Odeon Cinema. The construction of the cinema was underway when this photograph was taken between 1935 to 36. The contractors were John Williams Ltd, a local firm existing for many years in the Trewhiddle region of the town.

George Oliver's business at No. 22 Fore Street was described in the *Kelly's Directory* of 1910 as a boot dealer. The four members of staff shown here are surrounded by boots and shoes, all ticketed items in a vast array. Some prices are quite visible. Oliver's sign and shop still exists in Fore Street, the only one from the examples shown in this chapter.

Founded in the mid-1880s, Messrs Williams and Giles, monumental stone masons were at the junction of West Hill and Park Road. There were once seven craftsmen employed here, five of them are in the photograph. The premises later moved to a larger site near the old St Austell foundry and also took over the business of Doney and Watts in Truro Road. The firm designed and sculptured the granite war memorial erected on the north side of the parish church after the First World War.

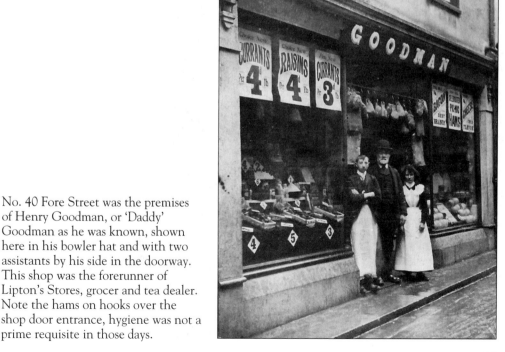

No. 40 Fore Street was the premises of Henry Goodman, or 'Daddy' Goodman as he was known, shown here in his bowler hat and with two assistants by his side in the doorway. This shop was the forerunner of Lipton's Stores, grocer and tea dealer. Note the hams on hooks over the shop door entrance, hygiene was not a prime requisite in those days.

This very old photograph tracing one of St Austell's earliest shop fronts was located on the corner of Fore Street and Church Street, where W.H. Smith's later stood for many years. Juleff & Co. were outfitters on the opposite side of the street and John Pooley was obviously proud to advertise that he had formerly been in their employ. The suits hanging outside the shop windows and the grand display of hats in the upper window emphasised that boaters were the gents' fashion of the day.

Three
Buildings

Walk through St Austell and there are still a number of fine buildings to be seen, many of them showing a date stone of their foundation. Always look up to the tops of buildings, above the street level, where many ancient outlines and fine architectural details are still evident. Most buildings featured here have changed their original function but the well-dressed, cut granite façades, windows and entrances still emblazon the skill of the stone masons of the nineteenth century.

A bill heading of F.E. Stocker, a well-established ironmonger and hardware business who sold everything from nails to iron bedsteads or a Cornish range.

The Town Hall and Market. Built in 1844 at a cost of £7,000, this was a new large market house for St Austell. It replaced an older one recorded on the site in 1791. The old market only held space for corn, potatoes, dairy goods and meat. White fish and vegetables were sold outside. By 1844, the 24 market commissioners had deemed that there was to be no more street trading in St Austell and the new building of local granite was completed. The vaulted ceiling in the entrance hall is still a fine feature to see together with the stone staircases to the main hall and gallery on either side of the building. The meat market and butchers' stalls were on the centre of the ground floor with occasional live animals on display in the alcoves around the walls. The main entrance was primarily for farm produce and on the first floor there were long benches for the farmers' wives to sell eggs, poultry, butter and jams. The meat market closed during the First World War and the Town Hall, which could seat from 300-400 people was converted to a cinema or picturedrome. The site is now an extensive hardware business. The Market House building was once used as the local fire station on the floor level with the road on the north side, and from the gallery, both Mr Gladstone and Winston Churchill addressed 8,000 people on separate occasions.

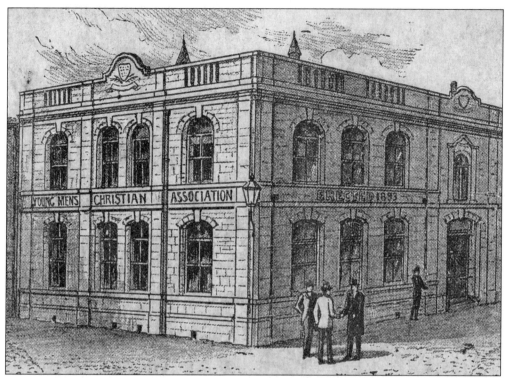

This building erected in 1893 on the site of
the Ring of Bells public house, which had
been demolished for the purpose, was the
first YMCA building in Cornwall. It
contained a gymnasium and reading room
and catered for the education and welfare of
the young men of St Austell. It was situated
on the corner of old Vicarage Hill and
Victoria Place and is now Frydays fish and
chip shop.

The Liberal Club situated at the end of Fore
Street was opened in July 1890. It was
erected solely by Francis Leyland-Barratt, JP
of Tregarne Lodge and was designed by
Silvanus Trevail. The ground floor
consisted of two shops, the first floor
contained reading and smoking rooms, a
library and kitchen while the second floor
had a large billiard room and secretaries'
office. There were about 400 members when
it opened, underlying the political
sympathies of the area and was said to be
the finest club house in the West of
England. The ornate front with its brick and
stonework is worth studying. The premises
are now 'The Thin End' restaurant.

St Austell County School was built in 1906, on new land at Poltair, a little way out of the town towards Tregonissey. The school was the new council school for secondary education in St Austell. It was a mixed school for pupils aged from 11-18 years. The granite frontage is surmounted by two fine sculptured badges, one of which is the county badge and the other is for the town (see Introduction), with the Cornish motto 'One And All' alongside. It is now part of Poltair Community School.

A rare view of the dining room of the St Austell County or Grammar School as it was later known. Generations of pupils ate their midday lunch here as many of them travelled several miles daily from outlying districts extending from Gorran Haven to St Dennis. The Venus de Milo bust in the far corner gazed serenely on many a lunch time fracas.

The girls' hockey team of the County School in 1925. Miss Parry stands at the back and the players are; back row, left to right: Edith Garner, Jean Kent, Phyllis Church, Mildred Paul. Middle row, left to right: Marian Best, Edith Paul, Mary Gale, Louise Williams, Florrie Matthews. Front row, left to right: Betty McTurk, Dulcie Rowett.

The St Austell County School, Tewington House in 1919. The teacher on the right was Gladys Medland. A.L. Rowse is in the back row, fourth from the left, next to tall Henry Pinch.

The Workhouse, built in 1839 replaced a former one which existed near the West Bridge. The new building was erected in part of the old Priory grounds at Sedgemoor and could accommodate 300 inmates. It was run by the St Austell Board of Guardians. The Union served the parish of St Austell from Tywardreath and Grampound to Roche.

Cottage Hospital, St. Austell.

This is probably one of the first photographs of the new cottage hospital built on Edgcumbe Road and opened in 1919. The hospital cause had been spearheaded by Harry Hodge and principal residents of the town. Annual fêtes were held at Trevarrick Hall with 4,000 people in attendance in 1928, and 'Hospital Saturday' continued for many years as the best fund raising effort. In 1920 a total of 165 patients were treated at the new hospital and 203 in 1921.

"Fairmead" Private Hotel, St Austell

Fairmead Hotel, situated in pleasant grounds at the junction of Palace Road and Carlyon Road was built soon after the Cornwall Railway had brought new prosperity to the town. It was converted to the offices of New Consolidated Mines of Cornwall Ltd, which owned works at Ponts Mill for several years, but was demolished in 1985 to make a site for the new St Austell Police Station.

Tremena House, known as 'Trelawney', was the home of F.E. Stocker, who owned the large ironmonger's shop in Church Street. It was a typical example of a fine town residence built during the era of prosperity which came to the town with the flourishing of the china clay trade. These large houses with indoor servants and gardeners ringed the town along the new routes and residential areas. This house was requisitioned by Sutton Boys' School from Plymouth during the Second World War, but before that had been an isolation hospital for scarlet fever and diphtheria. It was demolished in 1969 for building development.

St Austell Foundry was situated at the bottom of West Hill within the vicinity of 3 blowing houses for smelting tin. It was in existence before 1816 and in 1844, Mr John Hodge owned the St Austell iron and brass foundry principally for the production of mining machinery. He was listed as the engineer and iron founder. By 1883, William West owned the foundry premises as well as the one at St Blazey. An old catalogue lists 75 different cast iron items, all priced, and ranging from pistons and engine beams to tram wheels, stamp heads, anvil blocks, plough castings and shoes for wagon drags. In wrought iron, boilers and miners' shovels, kibble plates and chains were more costly.

From the top of West Hill the view dropped steeply to the foundry at its base. The St Austell Foundry stack is visible in this photograph. Lawley's china shop on the left was next to the ope way leading to Burton Place with its many small cottages. Next to the Baptist chapel was a lodging house owned by a Mrs Avery whose son Lewis was later a motor-cycle dealer in Slades Road. The Goodenough family business occupied the angled premises at the junction of Truro Road.

West Hill & Truro Road, St Austell.

Goodenough's family shoe business occupied this angular building at the junction of West Hill and Truro Road for 42 years until the 1960s road improvement schemes took place. Just below it in Truro Road was the Public Rooms or Assembly building erected in 1895 at a cost of £5,000. Here was room for special social functions, balls, dances, music festivals and operatic performances.

WORKS ALSO AT } Pydar St. & Richmond Hill, TRURO.
Station Rd. & Kimberley Rd, FALMOUTH

DONEY, SON, WATTS & TREVAIL, STATUARY MASONS.
West End ST AUSTELL Cornwall

Doney, Son & Watt's in Truro Road, was a fine, ornate building and the showroom of the business of monumental masons and sculpture. It was named 'a pavilion of sculpture and works of art'. The alcove above the main entrance can still be seen, minus the statuette. Celtic crosses for cemetery markers were displayed in the yard alongside.

43

The Sawle family of Penrice House were the chief landowners in the town. Formerly occupying Towan as head of the great manor of Tewington, the family moved in 1596 to rebuild and occupy Penrice. The present house dates from the eighteenth century and is a fine example of a mansion belonging to one of the gentry families. Throughout the nineteenth and twentieth centuries, the Sawle family were generous in their bequests of land and philanthropic concern for the welfare of St Austell. In 1971, when Mrs Rosemary Cobbold Sawle died, the house was converted to a residential home for the elderly.

Aylmer Place was a hodgepodge of cottages behind Fore Street with the backs of the cottages and shops jammed tightly together. This photograph shows the first stages of demolition in the 1960s to make way for the new Aylmer Square in the town centre.

The new town centre developed and built during the 1960s on land which included the car park for the Odeon cinema, Chandos Place, Aylmer Place and approaches from Fore Street. New shops were built in the pedestrian area, the Clifden Grill took over the first floor of these.

Trenance Mill situated at the foot of Blowing House Hill in the Trenance area of the town below Bodmin Road. From Carthew to St Austell there were five water wheels at one time, Trenance Mill had one of them. The building is now used by Francis Antony, a printers. Alongside was the wholesale provision merchants of Stephens & Pope Ltd who catered for most of the grocers in the town.

This view taken from the top of the Classic cinema in the 1960s shows the New Inn, the Bluebird Café and Chandos Place due to disappear in the redevelopment of the town.

Four
Parish Church and Chapels

Dating from 1259, when Bishop Bronscombe consecrated it, the parish church of the Holy Trinity in St Austell is a fine example of early church architecture. The sculptures on the tower and the outside walls are some of the finest in the county. Standing on an eminence at a crossroads in the centre of the town, the parish church has withstood and witnessed the many changes over seven hundred years.

There have been many non-conformist chapels in St Austell, built during the nineteenth and twentieth centuries, of which only two remain today. These played their part in the life of the town when feast day processions and parades made the St Austell Feast Week a grand occasion for celebrations.

Wm. Orchard and Son, 1888.

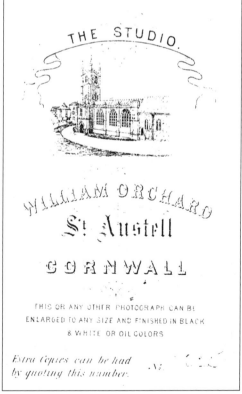

Wm. Orchard's business card.

The Parish Church in an 1834 view, taken from a coloured engraving showing the magnificence of the building at the centre of commerce in the town. Some of the trading and market transactions of the surrounding countryside took place at this time in the Bull Ring areas and around the church walls.

The Holy Trinity Church, an historic church built in 1259, is the oldest building in the town and is still used for its original purpose. This is one of the earliest photographs, taken in the 1880s, and shows a fine view of the church tower before the clock. A high wall marks the churchyard boundary on Market Street, the church vestry had not yet been built.

The Parish Church with a cobbled street and several bow-fronted shop windows in the 1830s.

The Parish Church covered with ivy and also showing the new vestry built on the north aisle, 1889. The new vestry cost £350 to erect and was donated in memory of Mrs Edmund Carlyon. The church clock with three faces was added in 1885 at a cost of £200.

PARISH CHURCH, ST. AUSTELL,   39

The Parish Church from a similar angle as the previous photograph but now with a circle of palm trees around it and the wall topped with iron railings. The White Hart sign is silhouetted against the sky. This area is now the site of the Bull Ring.

The interior of the Parish Church with the wonderful Cornish wagon roof with fine timbers and carved bosses.

The Parish Church viewed from the Tregonissey House area which shows the small shops and houses, which jutted out into Market Street in the early 1900s.

The interior of the Parish Church. An old view of the choir stalls, altar and east window, with the 1881 sculptured pulpit in the foreground.

The Holy Trinity, a magnificent group of figures on the western face of the tower which are carved out of Pentewan stone. The lowest tier has our Lord represented in the middle with the figure of St Austell on the right and St Mewan on the left. These two Celtic saints had churches established only 1½ miles apart.

St Mewan Parish Church, built on a sloping bank like the one at St Austell, has some Norman work but is mostly fifteenth century. There are six bells in the two-stage tower and the whole building is constructed from local granite.

St Paul's, the Parish Church at Charlestown. This parish was formed in 1846 from the larger one at St Austell. The church was built in 1851. The tower was not completed until 1971 when a new fibre glass spire was set on the tower, lowered into place by helicopter. The six bells were donated following an appeal, one of them by Noel Coward.

St John's Wesleyan Methodist Chapel. This building was erected on land given by the Sawle family and opened in 1828 with room for 1,000 sittings. It was restored in 1892 and was a very substantial, finely-built and equipped chapel. The eminent businessmen of the town and their families supported a three day bazaar in the Market House to raise £400 towards its restoration.

Bodmin Road and Wesleyan Church, St. Austell.

This entrance to St John's Methodist Chapel leads off the Bodmin Road. The fine granite posts and magnificent wrought iron gates lead on to a long drive approach.

The Bible Christian Zion Church. Early in the nineteenth century, the followers of William O'Bryan were meeting for worship on a site in Tregonissey Road using part of the Lecture or Assize Hall there. Conferences were also held there and such was the success of the denomination that in 1889 a new building was planned on an adjoining site. On 1 May 1890, the memorial stones were laid and by April 1891 the building was opened to accommodate 600 people. It had a very fine interior and Christian witness continued there for many years. The chapel closed on 28 August 1994 after the evening service.

The Friends Meeting House in High Cross Street. A beautiful mellow honey-coloured stone building, which dates from 1834, represents the Quaker religion in St Austell. This place of worship was built by the efforts of the Veale family of North Hill along with many other staunch business families of the same faith in the town. The graveyard alongside bears witness to the simple style of worship practised by the Quakers. A former burial ground at Tregongeeves, near the home of Loveday Hambly, was dissembled for road widening in the 1960s and stone memorial markers were brought to the Meeting House.

The Congregational Chapel in Duke Street. These premises were known as the 'Tabernacle' and had also been built on land belonging to the Sawle family. It was erected in 1850 on the site of an earlier chapel and the architect was Silvanus Trevail. The building could accommodate 350 people. There was a large Sunday school underneath. The chapel closed in the 1970s and was demolished to incorporate another entry to the new town centre.

A recently discovered photograph of the interior of the Congregational Chapel with the choir.

Charlestown Chapel, a fine mellow stone building, commenced in 1827 and completed in 1830, was erected on the site of an earlier Meeting House for the Methodists in the village. In 1808, Charlestown existed on the Lord's Day Plan of the St Austle Circuit. In 1889, the chapel was re-seated and a new rostrum built. It was a thriving place of Christian witness, serving its community in this important port near St Austell and continues as a place of worship to this day.

Bridge Methodist Chapel, situated in Mount Charles, a thriving centre on the outskirts of St Austell, was originally known as the United Methodist Free church. There was another Bible Christian chapel in Clifden Road, while the Wesleyan Methodists had another place of worship in Victoria Road. The Bridge Methodist chapel closed about 1980 and was demolished in 1985 to make way for housing development.

The St Austell Parish Church garden party, just before the First World War. The ladies of the town seemed to be vying with each other for the largest hat. The vicar was Revd W. Blackmore.

The Mount Charles Feast Day celebrations, c. 1895. This scene was typical of all Methodist Sunday school anniversary tea treats where the fine tea tables, laid with the best china and silver teapots, made a wonderful social occasion.

Five

Processions
and Occasions

Over the years, St Austell has witnessed many ceremonial occasions, demonstrations and marches. As an important town in mid-Cornwall, it has been used as a central meeting place for a variety of organisations when a parade through the town has been planned.

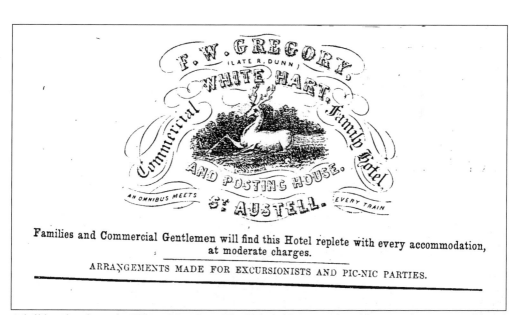

A bill headng from the White Hart Inn. The White Hart was the oldest coaching inn and hotel in the town. Formerly the town house of the Rashleigh family, it had been adapted to a hotel by the addition of another storey. The advertisement claims that an omnibus to bring travellers to the White Hart met every train.

A royal visit to St Austell. In 1909, the Prince and Princess of Wales, the Duke and Duchess of Cornwall, visited St Austell and the china clay works. There were ceremonial arches at both ends of the town to commemorate the visit. The one shown here is at the west end entrance to Fore Street. The car with the registration number AF 88 was a 12 H.P. De Dietrich and was owned by John Lovering of Cosgarne in 1904.

This second decorated archway was erected between the Corn Exchange and Coode's Bank in the Bull Ring area. The old post office, now Roy Dutch's camera shop, is visible through the archway, the lower part of East Hill is teeming with people.

This very patriotic banner was hung between two trees over some entrance gates along the route taken by the Prince and Princess of Wales. Three very elegantly dressed ladies pose in the gateway.

Coronation Day, 1911. A grand occasion in St Austell for wearing best clothes and celebrating. Fore Street is bedecked with flags and bunting strung from side to side. 'Long Live Our King and Queen' is on one banner.

Freemans Church Service, c. 1909. An unusual post card of Peace and Harmony Masonic Lodge members lining up outside the parish church after a thanksgiving service and before parading through the town. This was possibly the annual meeting of the Provincial Grand Lodge members.

The parade of the Freemasons through the town. The members of Peace and Harmony Lodge are in full masonic regalia after the service at the parish church.

A Sunday School Anniversary Feast Day Parade through the town at the turn of the century. The brass band always led the procession and then children, with banners, followed in the march around the streets. Stalls or standings lined the route.

The Clay Strike, 1913. This demonstration, led by the women, supported the decision to strike over union recognition and low wages in the clay industry. Wages were 18s a week, the men were striking for 25s minimum wage. The strike went on for eleven weeks. The procession is parading past the Public Rooms in Truro Road.

This card is labelled 'Suffragettes – 2nd visit to St Austell' and the occasion would have been pre-First World War. The lady speaker is fervently addressing the interested crowd from the railings around the church. The base of the tower is seen in the background. An older, well-dressed lady on the left is distributing tracts and maybe holding a collecting tin for the cause.

A very special occasion in the calendar of the church year. The ladies, who belong to the Girls' Friendly Society, are bedecked with decorative hats and fine clothes, in the wagonette outside the Parish church Sunday schoolroom in South Street before starting on their annual outing in 1909.

Another Feast Day Parade with a brass band leading a Sunday School march along Fore Street. This is an early photograph, c. 1887.

The British Red Cross in the 1940s. This parade of the St Austell detachment passing the White Hart was led by Dr K. Moore, the commandant in the centre foreground. She was the daughter of Dr Stephens, a well-known St Austell physician for many years. The three nurses behind her are, from left to right: Myrtle Reeves, (assistant commandant), Sister Batchelor from Pentewan and Miss Howell. A.G. Watkins, the chairman of the Urban District Council was alongside the platform where the station commander from St Eval is taking the salute.

Six

General Views
and Approaches

St Austell was built on the slopes of the hills leading down from the heights of Scredda and Carwollon right to the valley floor at Trenance. Fore Street was built around the side of a hill so was level but the other streets and roads leading to the town followed the incline of the slopes from the higher ground. Consequently, the views of the town are mostly distant ones from the approaching roads.

A bill heading from George Hawke & Son, 1910.

St.Austell, general view.

O2291.C

This view of the town was taken from the grounds of a property at the western end of St Austell. It shows how the town has spread around the gentle slopes with the church tower a predominant feature. The Public Rooms are clearly visible on Truro Road and the Baptist chapel at the head of West Hill with the buildings of West Hill school below.

From another direction in the East Hill area, this was a view of the town from the slopes of Carvath, looking towards the church. The chimneys of the workhouse or St Austell Union can be seen behind trees in the middle distance. Walter Hicks' steam brewery at Tregonissey House, built in 1869 on the site of the London Inn in Market Square, is also visible at the extreme right.

Palace Road, was a new road built and developed after the advent of the Great Western Railway from Plymouth into Cornwall in 1859. There were many fine residences built by the newly affluent china clay merchants or business families in the town, eg. Polgray, Methleigh and Trevarthian House. These were set back off Palace Road within their own spacious grounds.

King's Avenue, St. Austell.

King's Avenue, was another new road built to connect High Cross Street to East Hill after the development of St Austell railway station in 1884. The brick, granite-capped pillars fronted the entrances to substantial new detached residences. The trees standing on the left indicate that the ground there was still to be developed.

East Hill, St. Austell.

East Hill, the main thoroughfare or turnpike, as it was formerly known, climbed out of the town and on through St Blazey, Lostwithiel and Liskeard to Plymouth. This view was taken at the higher part of the hill with Beech Road on the left as a new development but the old houses on the right jutted out onto the road, with Paul's Square and Merrifield's tucked in behind.

Colenso Place, St. Austell.
(Council's Workmen's Dwellings).

Colenso Place, at the top of Eastbourne, just off Albert Road, was a new housing development in 1883. It was named after Bishop Colenso of Natal, born in St Austell and a noteworthy pioneer of Christianity in South Africa. These new council workmen's dwellings were a fine addition to the area in contrast to the cluster of old cottages opposite.

This ancient baptistry known as Menacuddle Holy Well is situated underneath a high wall on the Bodmin Road, just past the railway viaduct in the woodland below the Brake. The land was given to the people of St Austell by the Cobbold-Sawle family and the baptistry, which has a fine arched entrance and a spring of water, was restored by the Sawle family in memory of the heir who was killed at Ypres during the First Word War.

Menacuddle Bridge, a fine old granite structure of huge slabs over the St Austell river is almost hidden by foliage in the heavily wooded area of Menacuddle on the way to the Holy Well.

An aerial view of St Austell, which shows a good view of the town on the southern slopes of the hills. The bypass area of Penwinnick Road is visible in the foreground. The cross roads of Truro Road and Gover Road can be seen in the mid-distance. The railway viaduct, with the old pillars alongside, spans the Trenance Valley with the Brake in view just beyond. The clay tips of Greensplat, Cocksbarrow and Hensbarrow are clearly visible on the high granite moors in the distance. The old western turnpike approach to the town is hidden practically from view between the new Truro Road and Penwinnick Road.

An aerial view showing Moorland Road in the lower foreground in 1930. West Hill Secondary school is on the left hand side surrounded by its large school yard. Immediately behind the yard there are cows in pasture land which must surely have been the last field to remain before complete development took over. Gardens and allotments are much in evidence on the cultivated land leading down South Street.

An unusual sight in St Austell. This early thatched cottage, in the Pondhu Road was in the area where Mike Best's autospares premises are today.

Truro Road, St. Austell.

Truro Road, this gentle wooded approach to the town stressed the newly acquired wealth brought to St Austell by the growth of the china clay industry. Clinton, Caprera, Cosgarne and Belfield were substantial new dwellings in this area. In the foreground the clay wagon from the Trewoon area is using this new route into the town as opposed to the old one down a steep hill and through the grounds of Trevarrick Hall.

St Austell, Gorer Mill

Gover Mill in the Trenance Valley area of St Austell shows the very rural aspect of the town in the early days before housing development and traffic destroyed the established industries. Between Carthew and St Austell there were five working water wheels at one time. Note the huge overshot water wheel on the right hand side and the cluster of mill house workings.

Seven

Roads, Transport and China Clay

The system of roads around and through St Austell evolved like many other Cornish towns from the horse and cart era, when the stage coaches were the most important vehicles on the road.

The turnpike from Truro to Plymouth, Exeter and London, went through St Austell, hence the established coaching inns, the White Hart and the Queen's Head. New roads developed in the town as the wealth of the town increased and the coming of the Great Western Railway underlined the advent of tourism with its new demands on road systems and transport.

THE GARAGE,
BOSCOPPA,
ST. AUSTELL.

Nov 19th 1934

Mr L. Garner Garker

Dr. to W. P. COCKS,
CAR PROPRIETOR.

Open and closed
Cars for Hire.   TERMS MONTHLY.   Phone
St. Austell 388.

A bill heading from Percy Cocks, who owned the main taxi firm around St Austell from 1930 to the 50s. He had a fleet of immaculate vehicles, mostly Austin 18's.

This old granite bridge spanning the St Austell River had formerly carried all the traffic into the town, along the turnpike road. The roadway is only eight foot wide (2.4 metres) and an iron plate fixed to the side of the bridge in 1895 limited weight to the 'ordinary traffic' of the district. The bridge dates from the sixteenth century.

This earlier photograph of the old bridge at St Austell also shows the two sluice gates which were opened to feed the channels leading to the water wheel at Pondhu Mill. The line of stones in the foreground formed a barrier to dam the river to feed the sluice gates. Note the two old mill stones which may have been used for the same purpose on the dam.

During the construction of the bypass around St Austell in 1926 this bridge was erected on the Truro side of the Mevagissey roundabout. The clay laden White River or St Austell River was a mere trickle during the summer months when this work took place. The photograph shows the cut granite arch and the size of its span indicates the amount of manual labour involved. There is not a piece of machinery in sight. The labour-intensive workforce only needed Cornish shovels!

This part of the new St Austell bypass, to divert traffic from the narrow confines of Fore Street, was named Southbourne Road and Cromwell Road. Notice the wide grass verges which were left bordering the newly-built houses. The dip in the road is now the site of the roundabout for the Asda store.

Evan Gilbert Pugh was a baker who had premises on West Hill. This fine photograph shows his wagon advertising his trade as baker and confectioner, c. 1910. It was the custom for the town bakers and butchers to serve the outlying districts as well as the town residences.

William Avent was also listed in the *Kelly's Directory* of 1910 as a shopkeeper at Tregonissey. Here he is with his immaculate delivery wagon also advertised as baker and confectioner. The young helpmate is seated happily on the shafts with some refreshment, probably a saffron bun.

F.W. May, a butcher at the west end of town, owned a really smart butcher's van. This photograph taken outside the Fairmead Hotel in Palace Road, now the police station, shows the glass panels on the side displaying the meat, game and poultry. The butcher behind is holding a knife and sharpening steel, posing ready for his first customer.

W.H. Harris ran a famous establishment which was a posting and carriage business with stabling in the cobbled yard at the bottom of East Hill, which thrived and existed in the town for many years. He hired wagonettes, jingles, brakes and carriages for weddings, funerals and outings and the stables were used by visiting farmers on market days. In the photograph he is shown on a very smart, low carriage harnessed with a fine pair of greys.

A St Austell carnival float paused for this photograph next to the Corn Market corner. The carnival was held on the last Saturday in August for many years.

This vehicle in the station yard at St Austell, was one of the very early GWR buses. The sign in the near window shows that it is on the St Dennis route. The advertisement on the top is for T. Williams & Son, family butcher and game dealer and in the 1873 directory his premises were listed as No.8 Fore Street. There was seating both inside the bus and on the roof, reached by the spiral staircase, with the driver seated out in the open.

The St Austell Railway Station, c. 1885. A very early photograph showing the station yard with the waiting horse conveyances. There was no footbridge over the line at the far end by the signal box, only a level crossing which was replaced by the new footbridge in 1931. The first new building along Palace Road can be seen.

An early steam passenger train at the station in St Austell on the up line, while the goods' train is shunting back into the sidings just below Palace Road. In 1931, the goods' depot was transferred to yards at Polkyth.

This photograph taken from the garden of a house in Bodmin Road shows the old Trenance Viaduct over the valley. The inverted wooden trestles were fixed to granite pillars, the remains of which are still visible. This structure took the first single railway track to Truro and the West in 1859.

Another view of the trestle bridge carrying the railway line. This photograph was taken from the Gover side of the valley, probably in the grounds of the Brake. It shows the spread of St Austell in the distance with the church left of centre, the workhouse from the Bodmin Road end and open fields leading to the south coast.

The granite structure which replaced the first single line viaduct showed its imposing span from Truro Road. The fine shrubberies and trees in the gardens of the new homes built in Trevarrick spread across the foreground.

The Trenance Viaduct, viewed from the Bodmin Road. The camber of the road surface indicates the ever needful wariness for the two-way traffic, especially clay wagons with their pyramid loads of clay blocks. These would come from the Carthew, Ruddlemoor works on their way to Charlestown harbour for shipping. Supports of the first single line viaduct are visible alongside the newer one.

St Austell Bus Station in the 1950s. The Western National buses are in line in the station yard awaiting passengers. The siding line for goods' trucks across the bus depot shown here on the right, was lifted in March 1965. The buses were known as 'Bristols' and the second one shows the old model luggage rack on the roof.

The Motor Rail train from Paddington halts at St Austell Station in the mid-1970s. The passenger part of the train has stopped in the old goods' line area, from where the passengers are transferred to collect their cars on the main line. There were two train services every Saturday during the summer season and this was a popular and stress free way to reach the West Country.

84

No book on St Austell would be complete without a reference to the growth of the china clay industry. Conical waste sand burrows were once a common sight on the edges of the open cast pits which produced the clay. The waste material was taken from the pit bottom up the incline by trucks known as 'skips'. This one near St Austell still remains on the skyline.

CLAYWORKS NEAR ST. AUSTELL

These settling tanks of clay slurry pictured here in the early 1900s were built on the slopes of the Trenance Valley with St Austell in the distance. The clay, once separated from the water was channelled into the linhays or drying pans where fierce furnaces produced heat to dry out the clay and finish the process before transportation to the docks.

This very early photograph of china clay workers shows them taking out ground for the pans near a new mica linhay. In the background are the first type of air drying sheds where men are stacking the clay blocks.

Trucking Casked Clay.

From the 1840s until the 1940s, the finer grades of china clay were still being packed by hand. Cooperages in the St Austell area made casks in vast numbers like the ones pictured above, which have been brought to this linhay to be filled with clay. Each cask held 2cwt and once filled, they were rolled into the waiting railway trucks.

ST.AUSTELL: CHARLESTOWN HARBOUR, SHIPPING CHINA CLAY.

Charlestown Harbour. The inner basin of this thriving little port from the 1870s to the 1970s is shown above. The scene here illustrates the amount of heavy manual labour involved in transferring the blocks of clay from the wagons to the waiting ships. These were the type of horse-drawn wagons, a frequent sight in the streets of St Austell for over 100 years. Sometimes, the clay was loaded down the chute from the tramway, mounted on a gantry running along the roadside at the top of the docks.

This old engine was used in the yard at the terminus of the Pentewan railway, in St Austell at the foot of West Hill behind Moorland Road. The railway which ran from 1832 to 1918, transported the china clay in wagons to Pentewan some three miles distant. In the background are the old St Austell foundry buildings. Fond memories of older St Austellians included riding in the cleaned clay wagons on a Sunday School outing through the wooded valley to the Winnick at Pentewan. (Reference: *A Cornish Childhood* by A.L. Rowse.)

This Packard car once belonged to Sir John Keay. Here it is at Cosgarne in readiness for a trip to London. Sir John Keay was the company chairman of English Clays Lovering and Pochin, the large company of amalgamated groups, for over 30 years. The company's headquarters in St Austell at John Keay House was named after him.

Eight
Organisations
and Clubs

The range of social activities within the town was the result of enterprising individuals and a great community spirit. Men worked hard but found time to produce vegetable gardens, sing in a male voice choir, or join a brass band. St Austell boasted of many leisure activities, volunteer organisations and public events held annually.

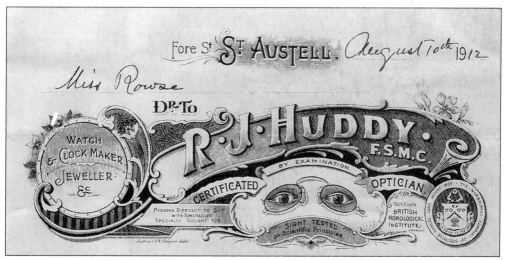

An advertisement for R.J. Huddy, certified optician.

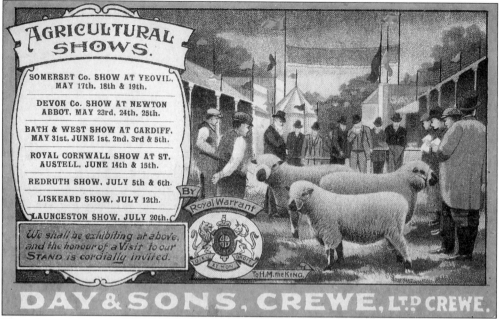

This advertising postcard of Day & Sons lists various agricultural shows. It pinpoints the Royal Cornwall Show when it was held at St Austell in 1911, in the fields lying to the south of the town. This show took place on different sites and towns in Cornwall and was held in St Austell on seven occasions between 1859 to 1954.

His Royal Highness the Prince of Wales inspected the Duke of Cornwall's Light Infantry on his visit to the Royal Cornwall Show in 1933.

The fields at Rocky Park, on the crest of the hill just before it descends towards St Mewan school, provided the venue for an airfield used by Captain Percival Phillips and F.H. Hill. The Cornwall Aviation Company was formed in 1924 and the bi-planes, pilots, engineers and stunt men provided hair-raising feats for the public on various occasions. The two men were partners of Hill and Phillips garage.

The St Austell Motor Club also made use of Rocky Park. The speedway programme was organised and held in St Austell during the years 1934 to 1938. Here we see Bill Kitchen, a famous speedway rider on this circuit during these years.

This photograph commemorates the opening of the new recreation ground or park at the western end of the town just below Truro Road. It was celebrated as an occasion of some importance as can be seen from the group shown here. The local town dignitaries, in top hats, with their ladies in flamboyant beribbonned bonnets, flanked Mr Harry Hodge in the centre.

RECREATION GROUND, ST. AUSTELL.

The park at St Austell was laid out with paths, shrubberies and flower beds to complement the Truro Road approach to the town. It was used a great deal at the turn of the century and was a pleasant rendezvous.

This magnificent scene outside the newly-built premises of Coode's bank reflected the popularity of the St Austell Cycling Club. This photograph was taken during the summer of 1898/9. Mr Fred Nicholls, who owned the jewellers at No. 29 Fore Street, and his wife are shown here with their bicycles and are marked with an x, first and seventh from the left hand side.

A view of produce and stalls on show one year at the St Austell Cottage Garden Society exhibition. This show was held annually in the Market House and attracted a great deal of interest and rivalry amongst local Cornish gardeners and estate managers. The society was formed in 1847. The structure of the hammer beam roof timbers was recognised as a marvellous feature of the building for its age, even more so as it still exists today.

St Austell Fire Brigade, a view that shows a very early fire appliance lined up with the volunteer firemen outside Trevarrick Hall, for a fire practice demonstration. Mr Harry Hodge, the owner of Trevarrick, is seen in the bowler hat alongside.

St Austell Volunteer Fire Brigade shown here in front of their horse-drawn fire engine and hose cart at Tregrehan Lodge, 9 May 1889. Back row, from left to right: A. Mitchell, Tom J. Smith, H. Bennetts, H. Hodge, T.J. Smith (Captain). Middle row: from left to right: F. Warne, F. Stephens, J. Tucker, E. Francis. Front row, from left to right: J. Jacob (Lieut), J. Hooper, J. McTurk, H. Williams, S. Bettison, A. Hart, W.G. Behennah, G. Nancollas. The man in the bowler hat was the engineer, J. Samble.

St Austell Volunteer Fire Brigade lined up in full uniform and brass helmets for this photograph taken in 1897. Captain Tom Smith was seated next to the driver, Assheton-Salton, who also serviced the new engine. Back row, from left to right: Howard Stephens, -?-. Middle row, from left to right: Captain T.J. Smith, Lieut W.A. Coon, Ronnie Nile, -?-. Front row, from left to right: Tom Sanders, Frank Blight, Cecil Rowse, George Thomas, Gordon Nicholls, Tom Williams, Walter Hoskin, Stuart Warne.

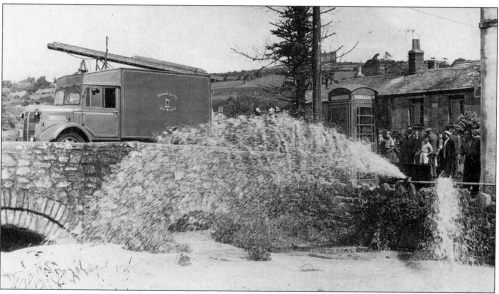

This is an unusual photograph of the St Austell or White River in flood at the West Bridge in the early 1950s. The ATV or Austin Towing Vehicle positioned on the bridge belonged to the Cornwall County Fire Brigade. The three arches of the bridge are scarcely visible, while from the standing pipes on the side more water is being pumped back into the river.

On 14 October 1940, a tremendous fire in Fore Street, St Austell, produced this dynamic photograph. The fire broke out in the boiler room of the Co-op shop, built by Mr Kirk of North Hill Park shortly before the start of the Second World War. The devastation caused a total blockage in the street after the collapse of much of the building. Howard Mills, who as a pupil at West Hill school, recalled seeing the fire brigade break the windows of the Bluebird Café to get access to water quickly. Some firemen are inspecting the damage off the Woolworth's flat roof.

A similar scene to the previous one but farther back in Fore Street towards the Parish Church. Spectators have gathered here, to inspect the damage and watch the action amongst the many hoses leading off in all directions. Mr Alf Wilson, the manager of Hodges is seen in the doorway of this shop while another shop assistant is giving a helping hand with the hose being taken up on the roof.

Another view of the fire at the Co-op building, looking towards the church.

A view of the fire from the area of the Odeon Cinema with the New Inn and Chandos Place.

The fire-damaged cottages in Chandos Place show the extent of the recent conflagration. The site of the Co-op was left derelict for many years and was considered an eye-sore in the town until a new development of shops was built in the 1960s.

St Austell AFC was established in 1890 and for the first few years played at Rocky Park, but soon moved to Poltair. This photograph of the St Austell AFC was taken in the 1924/25 season. The players were, back row: Mills. Third row, left to right: Marshall, Bray, Townsend. Second row, left to right: Smith, Turner, Husband. Front row, left to right: Rowe, Wembly, Tonkin, Webb, Wemyss.

St Austell Bowling Club, 1930. The bowling club at St Austell moved to these new premises at Poltair where a club house and fine green had been provided. A.G. Watkins is bowling in this photograph.

The St Austell Amateur Operatic Society, a thriving society right up to the present time and still producing an annual show is shown here in the 1917 production of *HMS Pinafore*. The cast were: Mr W.F. Rowe as Sir Joseph Porter, M. Norman Gilberte as Captain Corcoran, Mr Morley Richards as Ralph Rackshaw, Mr Tom Phillips as Dick Deadeye, Mr Joseph Hicks as Bill Bobstay, Mr Edwin George as Bob Beckett, Miss Dithe Smith as Josephine, Miss Nell Carter as Hebe, Miss Blanche Beattie as Little Buttercup. The musical director of this performance was Brennand Smith.

A production of *The Mikado* in 1930. The cast were: Mr. Julian Pascoe as The Mikado, Mr Morley Richards as Nanki Poo, Mr E.F. Robinson as Ko Ko, Mr F.R. Jago as Pooh Bah, Mr J. Kellow as Pish Tish, Mr H. Flynn as Go To, Mrs Reg Dyer as Yum Yum, Miss M. Venning as Pitti Sing, Mrs Legh Pope as Katisha, Master Gerald Nancollas as the Sword Bearer.

Nine

The District

From the centre of St Austell to the south coast at Charlestown and the higher quarters to the north, there were a number of small outlying settlements, hamlets or villages. Most of these were self-contained communities with shops, chapels and schools as the focal points. Rows of miners' cottages were added and with the development of a better road system, the outlying district became integrated into a much larger St Austell.

Tregonissey, St. AUSTELL,

.... **191**

ℳ ....

𝕭𝖔𝖚𝖌𝖍𝖙 𝖔𝖋 **R. ROWSE,**

GROCER AND TEA DEALER.

A bill heading from Richard Rowse. In the village of Tregonissey, one of the first small settlements travelling northwards from the town, Richard Rowse and his wife Annie owned a grocery shop. These were the parents of A.L. Rowse. The site of the shop is now Quality Box, Tregonissey.

Alexandra Road. From the East Hill, leaving the town of St Austell, the road continues into Alexandra Road or Watering Hill as it was previously known. This name evolved from the days of horse-drawn traffic, when the horses would stop for watering from the open river which flowed alongside Eliot Road. This river was culverted under Alexandra Road and continued as an open river again in Woodland Road. The development of stone-fronted houses with bay windows dates from the turn of the century. There was no Capitol Bingo Hall built when this photograph was taken.

This photograph was taken from the lower end of Alexandra Road looking up towards the town. The grocery shop and general store on the left belonged to W. and F. Higman for over 30 years, then it was run by M. and P. Jacob and family until 1974. It is now Varkers Domestic Appliances. In the wall, on the right hand side, a granite alcove contained a tap, the community water supply for several households before the council brought water into the houses.

102

Laying pipes alongside the road in Watering Hill, as shown on the postcard, before houses numbered 120 and 122 were built.

Simon Jenkins lived at the bottom of Alexandra Road on the corner with Woodland Road. He stored old cars in what is now the Capital bingo hall car park, just alongside the railway arch at the bottom of Eliot Road. The mechanics posed for the photograph in this ramshackle old convertible, possibly with faulty brakes. Note the stone under the rear wheel.

The view in Mount Charles along Victoria Road coming from St Austell. The old Silvanus Trevail Wesleyan Methodist chapel of 1873, on the left hand side, had an imposing façade of honey-coloured brick, with windows outlined in red brickwork. It was demolished in 1995 and rebuilt as the new Mount Charles Methodist church. The cottages and line of shops on the left are still unchanged.

A lovely scene in Mount Charles with two trundling clay wagons proceeding to Charlestown harbour. The couple in the horse and cart were overtaking the slower wagons. There is not much fear of oncoming traffic! The cottages on the left, built right out onto the road, were demolished in the 1960s.

Mount Charles had developed and by the 1900s was a busy thoroughfare, especially at the junction of the road to Bodmin. This photograph taken just outside the Duke of Cornwall Inn was the feast day march, of the anniversary of a local Sunday school, led by a brass band. The new walls of shops and houses are being built on the left, with stalls or standings, typical of all feast day celebrations, along the roadside.

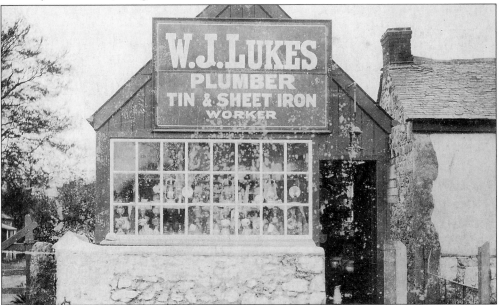

A hitherto undiscovered postcard of the small shop owned by W.J. Lukes, plumber, at No. 19 Mount Charles Road. It is a classic example of the well-stocked ironmongery shop of its day. Notice the hurricane and oil lamps in the window. The shop was later bought by T.H. Mills in 1936 for the sum of £50, 'the agreed purchase price for plumbers shop together with fixtures and fittings, stock in trade and tools.' It is now owned by the Byrne family and run as a green grocery and garden shop.

At the other end of Clifden Road, from the crossroads at the Duke of Cornwall, was Cundy's garage. The barns and farm outbuildings were on the road side above Sandy Hill. The whole site is now taken over by Cornish Ford. The building in the centre owned by Mr Bohemia gave its name to the corner for many years.

The view down Sandy Hill from Treleaven's Cross, shows rough hedges and no development leading to the farm on the left. It is traffic free and there are no pedestrians in the quiet backwater leading to the village of Bethel.

Trelawney Road which connects Slades Road with the village of Tregonissey was built about 1910 and was known as New Road for some time. *A Cornish Childhood* by A.L. Rowse describes life in his village of Tregonissey at the turn of the century and beyond.

From Treleaven's Cross, the road through Slades led to Bugle, Bodmin and the 'Higher Quarters'. This view, before the building of the council houses, showed tree-lined gardens. The premises half way down on the left was the grocery store of Warwicks and is now Spar.

Tregonissey, St. Austell.

Tregonissey Lane End, the crossroads much as it is today minus the traffic lights. The shop and post office in the centre was run by the Kelley family for many years at the turn of the century. Carclaze chapel is seen up the hill on the right.

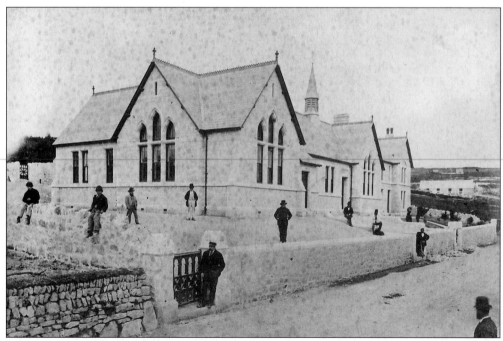

The Carclaze Board School built in 1880 and shown here not long after its opening. A building of fine structure, it had the headmaster's house at the far end. Children from Trethurgy two miles away walked there daily. It was the elementary school which A.L. Rowse attended from 1908 to 1914, before winning the scholarship to the County school.

This magnificent hive of industry featured the forge and wheel wrights business, at Tregonissey Lane End, owned by brothers Charlie and Tom Mitchell. The old cast iron road sign, to Bodmin, points uphill to Carclaze. Note the cast for wheels. The premises have been converted to a dwelling called 'The Old Forge'.

From Tregonissey Lane End the road led up Fourstones hill to the outlying village of Trethurgy. The building on the right was the stone crushing plant for the Carn Grey quarry opposite.

This scene through Tregonissey village shows the road as barely a lane with its hedges and fields of Lostwood overlooking the bay, c. 1909. The nearer shop was owned by the parents of A.L. Rowse, with his Uncle Rowe's china shop next door. This photograph shows A.L. Rowse aged 6 years old standing by the bush in front of the porch on the left with his brother.

Holmbush developed as a small thriving community of miners' cottages to house the men who worked at the Bucklers, Cuddra and Pembroke mines. The Holmbush Reading Room was erected by the hedge just behind the group in the foreground and is still there as the premises of Clemos.

Ten
The Coast

The south coast of Cornwall is about 3 miles from St Austell, the town which gives its name to St Austell Bay. The headlands on either side are the Gribben, with its red and white Trinity House shipping marker, and the Blackhead, seemingly always the colour of its name as it is formed from black volcanic rock.

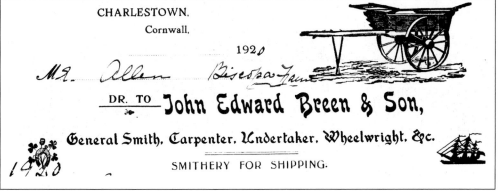

A bill heading for John Breen & Son, from Charlestown.

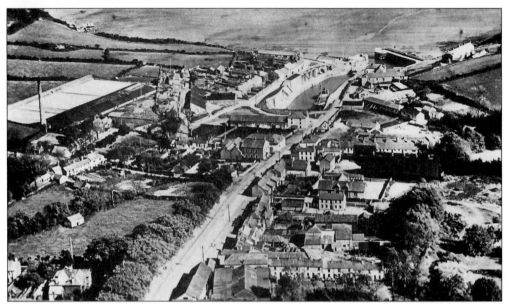

An aerial view of Charlestown, the little Georgian village, the nearest port to St Austell. It blossomed from a small fishing settlement of Polmear into a thriving port due to the enterprise of Charles Rashleigh. The harbour was the first development in 1791, formerly boats had been beached on the shingle cove, so when the inner basin was cut from the solid rock and sealed by lock gates permanent sheltered berths were available.

The Charlestown Hotel, c. 1885. This was situated on the way down to the harbour. The porch is still there and is now the entrance to the Rashleigh Inn. The Wesleyan chapel next door dates from 1821. Note the badly torn surface of the road by wheels of china clay wagons.

A view from the coastal footpath leading to the Gun Battery looking down into the harbour and inner basin, during the last days of the coastal trading ships. The content pilchard cellar is on the extreme right, with the china clay dries nearby, a symbol of the two Cornish industries.

Charlestown Dock, c. 1914. The towering masts of the trading vessels in the dock etched the skyline at Charlestown for over 150 years. The black gates, worked by the capstans, sealed the inner basin. The line of cottages above have fortunately remained almost unchanged even today.

A quieter scene of Charlestown Docks in 1939. Here we see the basin with three coastal vessels, topsail schooners, having brought in coal or timber and are safely anchored here. The iron capstans and poles which opened the dock gates are in evidence in the foreground.

A close-up view of the everyday scene on the dock, filled to near capacity, when horse-drawn wagons drew the huge blocks of clay from the dries to the ships. The wooden chutes, which often loaded clay straight into the ships' holds, are visible on the wall.

A delightful scene in the harbour on a regatta day, during the 1890s. The different types of craft are being appreciated by the scores of sightseers lining the pier. An early steam ship is anchored outside the mouth of the harbour while the tug in the entrance is towing the sailing vessel out.

Charlestown. Harbour Entrance.

The *Lady Sophia*, a trading vessel entering the dock in the 1950s. Even these small coastal vessels had to be carefully manoeuvred according to the state of the tide.

Crinnis Sands after the completion of the new Carlyon Bay Hotel in 1930. There was only a rough track, down over the cliffs to the beach, which led to the tennis courts and a small beach café. The island in the middle gave its name to the beach, Caer-enys. ('Enys' is the Cornish word for island.)

A close up view of the tennis courts and putting green near the café on Crinnis beach developed for the use of hotel guests. The beach was also gaining in popularity for picnics on Bank Holidays by the locals.

Crinnis Beach, shewing Hotel.

The building being erected near the cliffs at the back of the beach is now known as the Coliseum. It originally provided indoor sports facilities and an outdoor swimming pool filled with sea water for the guests at the Carlyon Bay Hotel. During the war it was used for storage purposes by the Ministry of Supply, then later an entertainment centre/night club/concert hall.

St. Austell Bay Hotel.
Par. Cornwall.

The new Carlyon Bay Hotel with no traffic in sight. It was an imposing structure on the cliff and offered luxury. King Edward VIII and Wallis Simpson once stayed here. There was a private golf course nearby and the London train was met at Par daily.

Another view of the hotel with the river carrying china clay waste from inland areas across the beach and into the sea. Here it very obviously covers a wide expanse of the bay.

In May 1940, the Canterbury Cathedral schoolboys were evacuated to the Carlyon Bay Hotel. They used the hotel for accommodation along with the Cliff Head Hotel opposite (then known as the Bayfordbury) and also made use of the squash and tennis courts on the beach. A few boys lodged at 'Carne' Private Hotel in St Blazey and sang at evensong in St Blazey parish church. Some classes were held at Trenarren House where the headmaster Canon Shirley made his home.

Duporth House, built by Charles Rashleigh in the early 1800s, was a unique Georgian residence of Pentewan stone and situated in timbered park land with gardens, terraces, coach houses and a fine clock tower. The house was later bought by Henry Hodge but demolished in 1988, when some of the stone was used for National Trust properties, one being Antony House, Torpoint. The site now belongs to Haven Leisure.

A view of the beach at Duporth, on the western side of Charlestown, with the cliff tops and fields still undeveloped in the 1930s. The beach was for private use for residents at Duporth House.

A Porthpean aerial view of the beach and part of the village including the church of St Levan. The approach to the beach was dominated by the extensive buildings used by the pilchard fishermen whose several boats are evident pulled up on the foreshore. The line of bathing huts on the beach is an indication of the growing popularity of sea bathing. This was always the bathing beach most popular for the St Austell people.

An unusual scene for Porthpean with a huge catch of mackerel which has been landed on the beach in the seine net.

Local fishermen straining to pull in the seine net on to the beach and watched by an interested group of women and children. The white-haired elderly lady holding the net in one hand has an early type of Kodak folding box camera which used 116 film and produced postcard sized photographs.

A scene of the net after it has been beached with a tremendous catch of mackerel. Two willow mauns are being loaded on the left. Note the early type bathing costumes

A wide expanse of Porthpean beach on a beautiful, calm, windless summer's day in the early 1900s. The rocks are covered with people hoping to catch the sun. This is the view from the garden of Porthpean House probably on a regatta occasion, with a grouped selection of stalls at the back of the beach to celebrate the holiday.

Porthpean House was the home of the Petherick family for over a hundred years. The Dolphin Inn was the original building and the two wings added by the Petherick family made an imposing residence overlooking the bay. Mr Maurice Petherick was a Conservative Member of Parliament for many years.

A row of six fishermens' cottages, now long demolished, were once built at the foot of the hill on the turning to the beach. The modern car park at Porthpean is now opposite the site of these cottages. The headland of Carrickowel is seen towering above the chimneys.

The Axford family were boat owners on Porthpean beach in 1910 and the tradition continued in the family for many years. A notable character was Charlie Axford shown here in front of the boathouse.

Lobb's Shop, this thatched cottage and blacksmith's shop was on the road from Porthpean to Pentewan at the Trenarren and Towan crossroads. Notice the ancient motor cycle, the dovecotes over the stable door entrance and the single shutters on the lower windows.

Trenarren village was the next place along the coast from Porthpean and was mostly owned by the Hext family, as it still is today. It is situated on either side of a sheltered and wooded coombe, running down to a little beach called Hallane.

This photograph, taken from a viewpoint halfway down the valley to Hallane, shows the mill with its waterwheel on the side, nestling in the hollow. The mill pool opened by sluice gates, let the mill race work the mill wheel. The ruins of the pilchard cellars can be seen above the beach.

Hallane beach is situated under the shelter of the Vans, a tremendously high cliff bulk with remains formerly of Iron Age fortifications. The leat, which led from the mill pool, diverted the water onto the beach throughout the year. The natural arch is still there and provides photographers with some spectacular shots even today when the tide and wind combine.

The Blackhead guards the western end of St Austell Bay and is a prominent 'humped' feature along the coast. The headland was the site of an Iron Age cliff castle.

A.L. Rowse is pictured here as a young boy at Tregonissey with his Grandmother and Grandfather Rowse. Neddy the donkey and cart were used for delivery to the lodge at Tregrehan.

Trenarren House built in 1805 is a small manor house at the head of the valley. It is the property of the Hext family and has been the home of Dr A.L. Rowse for nearly 45 years.

Dr A.L. Rowse, C.H., the Cornish author, poet and historian of Elizabethan studies, seated on the terrace at Trenarren in 1986. He is the most renowned St Austellian scholar of this century ranking among the literary giants of Oxford and Cambridge as the most distinguished of living Cornish literary men. He was the youngest ever don to be elected a Fellow of All Souls, Oxford.

This photograph, one of the oldest amongst this collection was taken in 1878 and shows the premises of W. and T. Sanders, printers of Vicarage Hill. The firm printed the *St Austell Star* newspaper. T. Sanders is standing in the middle of the group, W. Sanders is standing on the right.

The Sanders Dance Band in 1912. A St Austell dance band to play the finale. Back row, from left to right: ? Tamblin, Arthur Dunn, E.F. Robinson, S. Truscott. Front row, from left to right: ? Dunn, J. Sanders.